Figures
for the Ghost

Figures
for the Ghost

POEMS BY

Scott Cairns

The University of Georgia Press

ATHENS AND LONDON

Published by the University of Georgia Press

Athens, Georgia 30602

© 1994 by Scott Cairns

All rights reserved

Designed by Betty Palmer McDaniel

Set in ten on thirteen Trump Mediaeval

by Tseng Information Systems, Inc.

Printed and bound by Thomson-Shore, Inc.

The paper in this book meets the guidelines for
permanence and durability of the Committee on
Production Guidelines for Book Longevity of the
Council on Library Resources.

Printed in the United States of America

98 97 96 95 94   P   5 4 3 2 1

Library of Congress Cataloging in Publication Data

Cairns, Scott.

Figures for the ghost : poems / by Scott Cairns.

p. cm.

ISBN 0-8203-1601-6 (pbk.: alk. paper)

I. Title.

PS3553.A3943F54   1994

811'.54—dc20

93-11283

British Library Cataloging in Publication Data available

for Marcia

and for our children,
Elizabeth and Benjamin

*The apparition of God to Moses began in light;
afterwards God spoke to him in a cloud;
and finally in the darkness.*

—GREGORY OF NYSSA

Acknowledgments

The author and publisher gratefully acknowledge the
following publications in which some of the poems were
first published:

The Journal: "Advent"
Kansas Quarterly: "The Holy Ghost"
The New Republic: "The Death of Penelope," "Herod," "Dead
Sea Bathers"
The Paris Review: "Inscription," "And Also from the Son,"
"Mortuary Art"
Tampa Review: "Serenade"
The Wallace Stevens Journal: "The Glass Man"

The middle section of this collection first appeared as a
limited-edition chapbook, *Disciplinary Treatises,* published
in 1993 by Trilobite Press.

Contents

LATE EPISTLE

Figures
for the Ghost

Inscription

After the plague had come and gone a second time,
after the panic, after the convulsive festival,
after the silence had set in a second time,
I was astonished to observe I was still standing.

And there were one or two others in my region
similarly astonished and similarly
alone, but we kept apart, preferred not to tempt
fate—as it were—preferred this monastic enterprise,

which we, I suppose, undertook in a mixture
of mute relief and nagging culpability.
Nor did I presume the serpentine contagion
had withdrawn completely. The last outbreak had laid

a great litter of corpses, some of which yet offered
trembling carrion to what few corruptible
beasts survived with strength enough to forage still.
Along every path, at the edge of every

stubble field, anonymous remains flourished,
tattered like springtime gardens after rain. And one
knew better than to enter any darkened dwelling,
aware of what surely lived there now. I drew

my shelter from the mud and stone far from any road,
any chance for intercourse, and lay me down within,
having resisted just long enough to engrave
my puzzlement, this witness, in a likely rock.

Murmur

The Holy Ghost

Don't worry about it. Other figures would serve as well,
so long as they too imply the sort of appalling stasis
which still provokes unseen, albeit suspected, motion:
a murmur caught in the throat, heart's stammer, vertigo.

A windmill! Now that's lucky. But only if the rope is
secure which holds the lead blade to the anchor,
only if, against the fiercest gale, the blades cannot turn,
though they tremble, though they threaten even to come
   crashing

down, or to be torn away, carried—perhaps spinning now
and deadly—to some murderous reunion with the earth.
Well, that's a little theatrical, but you see what I mean.
The issue is the flight one's mind provides while influenced

by that shuddering stillness making itself . . . what? Supposed?
There were so many distractions along that narrow bay,
so many nearly invisible coves you would not find
unless your boat was slow enough let you trace the seam.

My fortune was the little coracle I had occasion
to row across the inlet. In retrospect, the chore
appears habitual, as if whole seasons had been measured
by my pulling against my grip on the chirping oars,

watching my wake's dissolution, its twin arms opening
to a retreating shore. And, true enough, I may have crossed
that rolling gulf many times each day in fair weather. Still,
I suspect this part I remember best happened only once:

I am rowing steadily enough, davening across
that bay and reaching the choppy center where I pause,
ostensibly to rest. But the breeze also stops, and a calm
settles upon those waters so suddenly I worry

for my breath, and can hardly take it in. And I am struck
by a fear so complete it seems a pleasure,
and I know if I were to look about—though I know better
than to try—I would find the circle of shoreline gone,

and myself adrift in an expanse of stillest waters.
Well, it didn't last. A little air got in, and I sucked it up,
and the boat lifted, almost rocking, across a passing swell.
The shoreline was called back to its place, its familiar shape,

and there were people on it, and I think a couple dogs.
So I kept rowing, though I wouldn't remember until
I'd docked the boat why I'd made the trip. It was an errand
to call my brother back from swimming, which I did.

Return Directive

Back out of all this now too much for us . . .

The road there—if you take the road and not
the shorter, crude diagonal that cuts
across a ruined and trampled pastureland—
is nearly winding as a spiral stair.

Wind there neither flags nor any longer
rages as a fabled wind might have done;
the winding road grants progressive, hidden
groves where you might find standing still

a profitable diversion from what
journey you thought to take, and each of these
may disclose a path or two—game trails,
but I think more than game might find some use

in taking one. Such a path I'm guessing
may never bring you back, but will demand
another turn, in turn, another choice,
and you will choose and walk, choose and pause.

If lost at all you're lost to those behind you;
to what's ahead you're a kind of imminence.
Besides, whatever loss or gain others
measure, you will know what line you travel

and, if you live and move, how far, how well you fare.

Prospect of the Interior

A little daunting, these periodic
incursions into what is, after all,
merely suspected territory.

One can determine nothing from the low
and, I'm afraid, compromised perspective
of the ship, save that the greenery is thick,

and that the shoreline is, in the insufficient
light of morning and evening, frequently
obscured by an unsettling layer of mist.

If there are inhabitants, they've chosen
not to show themselves. Either they fear us,
or they prefer ambush to open threat.

We'd not approach the interior at all
except for recurrent, nagging doubts
about the seaworthiness of our craft.

So, as a matter of course, necessity
mothers us into taking stock of our
provisions, setting out in trembling parties

of one, trusting the current, the leaky
coracle, the allocated oar.

The Glass Man

He is the transparence of the place in which
He is . . .

This is where he washed to shore
during rough weather in November.
We found him in a nest of kelp,

salt bladders, other sea wrack—
all but invisible through
that lavish debris—and we might

have passed him by altogether
had he not held so perfectly
still, composed, so incoherently

fixed among the general
blowziness of the pile.
Unlikely is what he was,

what he remains—brilliant,
immutable, and of speech
quite incapable, if revealing

nonetheless. Under his foot,
the landscape grows acute, so that it seems
to tremble, thereafter to dissolve,

thereafter to deliver to the witness
a suspicion of the roiling
confusion which brought him here.

Serenade

The Past? I held it only briefly, but it was mine.
Evenings with The Past were best of all: so much
of the day behind us,

so little left, she would undress by candlelight
(we all had candles then; I'm talking about The Past),
and she was pleased to stand

a long while before me—too long, really—accepting
my eye and the warm swelling of the room, savoring
the wonder of her flesh,

its momentary, astonishing colors pulsing.
Then, the bedclothes, the ribbon at her thigh, the fire
of each trembling candle,

the murmuring of what seemed music in my throat—
all wavering as she like a wave opened
over me and we met.

That was the gift of The Past to me, earlier
version—less elaborate, less mediated
life—but a version without

which I could not be: fragrant oil of The Past, ache
and arc of a reflected radiance, umber
flame coloring our selves.

The Death of Penelope

She went, as you would guess, in her famous,
perversely faithful bed, alone, longing
for her lost boy (wandering desperately
God knows where) her absent daughter (hostage
to a grieving, all-but-luckless suitor,
a petty, hostile man, by all accounts,
incapable of gratitude for what
little luck he onetime must have held)
and longing, if only a little less,
for the hero, long estranged and never
heard from after parting for "one last journey"
to plant an oar in some flat wilderness.
One supposes the clever man must have run
clean through his gamut of tricks, and run out
of stories too, perhaps, as he lay face
down in a stony, treeless field, far from home,
his vast holdings, but approaching the deep,
unpleasant laughter of the inside,
oracular joke, witnessing the dissolve
of all topography, finding against
his face the grinning abyss, himself
unable to let go the little oar.

But as the woman lay dying, for whom
the many-passaged myth was always her
own story, as she lay tasting this new,
sudden pain, which took each harshest, prior
trial and made each a mere cordial
leading to this full draught of bitterness,
just as she glanced about, about to find
herself finally overrun with sorrows,

she found across the room's pure air her loom,
emptied of work, bright with erasure,
bearing only the nothing that suggests,
in its blank face, an approaching visage,
in its stillness, a note rising, as she
fully consumed by pain also rises,
imagines she stares back reading her long
tale of vacancies, pattern of absence,
and constructs of these a new, a stranger
story, now commencing. As the faithless
body and its weakness for toleration
fall finally to the misshapen tree,
Penelope rises, lets fall her dress,
begins the journey, nothing in her hands.

Herod

The murder of sons? Egyptian motif,
a taste I acquired with the throne—
expedient in the extreme.
Naturally, I began with my own:

Two sons, left alone, become two kings.
Could you expect me to leave them alone?
I've learned what lasts if I've learned at all.
Dead sons, granted, but with a note of renown.

As for my mother? And my wife? Harmless?
Such wombs make kings, save in the tomb.
Shall we say I helped them be harmless?
These chambers are cold; I keep warm.

Regrettable measures, perhaps, but taken;
all of which has left me quite alone.
Hence the two hundred—all of them sons,
bound by the sword to batten down

this monument, to lend a more enduring
radiance, even now, to my pyre.
See how its heat consumes each century,
how these embers dance—music of my fire—

and tender a fair host of mourners
into the bargain. So, the removal of sons
and of the threat of sons? One way to honor
the otherwise forgettable, all my own.

And when Israel is dust, when the weather
of ages erodes the holy in their bins,
I daresay you will remember, with these,
forever my offering to the innocents.

Advent

Well, it *was* beginning to look a lot like Christmas—
everywhere, children eyeing the bright lights and colorful
goods, traffic a good deal worse than usual, and most adults in
view looking a little puzzled, blinking their eyes against the
assault of stammering bulbs and public displays of goodwill.
We were *all* embarrassed, frankly—the haves *and* the have-
nots—all of us aware something had gone far wrong with an
entire season, something had eluded us. And, well, it was
strenuous, trying to recall what is was that had charmed us so,
back when we were much smaller and more oblivious than not
concerning the weather, mass marketing, the insufficiently
hidden faces behind those white beards and other jolly gear.
And there was something else: a general diminishment whose
symptoms included the *X*s in Xmas, shortened tempers, and
the aggressive abandon with which most celebrants seemed to
push their shiny cars about. All of this seemed to accumulate
like wet snow, or like the fog with which our habitual
inversion tried to choke us, or to blank us out altogether, so
that, of a given night, all that appeared over the mess we had
made of the season was what might be described as a nearly
obscured radiance, just visible through the gauze, either the
moon disguised by a winter veil, or some lost star—isolated,
distant, sadly dismissing of us, and of all our expertly
managed scene.

City Under Construction

As you might suppose, the work was endless. Even when
at last the City stood gleaming like flame in the troubled
radiance of that distended sun, we could not help but be drawn
to where our next project should begin: The loosening bolt,
flaking surfaces, another unnerving vibration in the yawning
superstructure.

We made a joke of it: The Eternal City! And let our lives run
out reworking the old failures, refining our materials, updating
techniques, but always playing *catch-up* to a construction that
just wouldn't hold, fretwork that wouldn't stay put, girders
complaining under the accumulating matter of successive
generations and an unrelenting wind.

Granted, it could have been worse; at least the work served as
an emblem of perpetual promise as every flagging strut
commenced another stretch of unquestioned purpose—
mornings when we rose from our beds eager and awake,
thoroughly enjoyed our food, and hurried out to work.

Nor would it serve to slight the rich *pathos* we shared like a
warming drink with co-workers. For there we'd be—touching
up the paint or turning that heavy wrench for
the hundredth time—and we'd smile, shake our heads
theatrically, say to each other how our City was *insatiable.*

Just the same, this was not precisely what we had intended—
that our City should grow into a self-perpetuating chore.
Earlier, we had imagined—more or less naively—a different
sort of progress, one with a splendid outcome. We fancied a

final . . . *conclusion,* from which we would not be inclined
to retreat.

I recall how, long before we had so much as made a start,
before we had cleared the first acre or drawn the first plan, we
saw the City, and as near completion then as it would ever be,
infinite in the best sense, its airy stone reaching to the very
horizon, and—I think this is the issue—extending
invisibly past.

The Lie of the Future

Some fictions are so pretty you may need to work
an entire lifetime to make up any ground at all,
any real progress against the good intentions
of mad inventors. *The Future,* for one—

tough little brick of a lie, imaginary
road paved with stolen pieces of our puzzlement:
the glib calendar and its rows of blank boxes,
unlikely schemes of lovers, mortgages.

They suggest the dim speculations of the blind,
slender constructions something like the pretty charts
Spanish explorers might have fashioned from thin air.
Except that the world, in this case, *is* flat.

Advance men have peopled it already, arranged
its militant forces and its architecture.
They've established its currency, levied taxes,
left you the bill, already overdue.

And still, *The Future* remains the one eternal
uncreated. It's not waiting, I think. It's just not.

The History of My Late Progress

First, what you might call the odd shoe dropping:
the mid-life (well, not—it turns out—*mid*-life)
heart attack, not massive by clinical
standards, but a close call what with fumbling
technicians, a rough ride to emergency.
I thought I was a goner.
                       Not really.
No one, I guess, ever really thinks that.
The closest we come is this uncanny,
dispassionate sitting-back, just watching
to see how we'll be saved. And then I was.
It was hard work for all of us, and hard
work for me thereafter,
                           tasting the new
bitterness—that any of this could end.
My *somatic* recovery advanced
passably. I agreed to medication,
certain and acceptable restrictions:
diet, activity, and so on.
I agreed to continue
                     as if I'd gained
new enthusiasm for simple things
like fishing, breathing, looking around.
Still, I'd been struck—apparently mid-stride—
by a little surprise. As *that* chagrin
faded, as the dose of bitterness sank
from memory,
                  I recalled something else.
Dying (even if I hadn't died, I'd
been dying) had an unexpected slant.
I mean, granted, I had watched those doctors,

19

their technicians, caught up, extravagant
in their procedures—each of them of *huge*
interest—
　　　　　but *I* was interesting too.
Oddly unafraid. Troubled, but eager.
It is my eagerness *then* which troubles
me now, the exotic thought that I was
more than just willing to see what would come.
Still, recovery is never complete,
which is just as well.
　　　　　　　　And in recent years—
the interim—other developments:
diabetes, The Big C (here, then there),
heart surgery. Each brought its own, extreme
demands, new chores, graceless dispensations.
Finally, one's late sentiments catch up
to what the body has
　　　　　　　　long determined.
Time. Time out. There has been labor here; one
prefers to imagine there is a style
of progress even after . . . after here.
So, with the merest supposition, I
proposed to recover something I had
lost, had relinquished,
　　　　　　　　now just suspected,
and in my so far severed circumstances
found agreeable, vast, beckoning.

The Beginning of the World

In the midst of His long and silent observation of eternal
presence, during which He, now and again, finds His own
attention spiraling in the abysmal soup, God draws up what
He will call His voice from unfathomable slumber where it lay
in that great, sepulchral Throat and out from Him, in what
would thereafter be witnessed as a gesture of pouring, falls the
Word, as a bright, translucent gem among primal turbulence,
still spinning. Think this is evening? Well, that was night. And
born into that turmoil so bright or so dark as to render all
points moot, God's pronouncement and first measure.

But before even that original issue, first utterance of our great
solitary, His self-demarcation of Himself, before even that first
birth I suspect an inclination. In God's center, something of a
murmur, pre-verbal, pre-phenomenal, perhaps nothing more
disturbing to the moment than a silent clearing of the
hollowed throat, an approach merely, but it was a beginning
earlier than the one we had supposed, and a willingness for
something standing out apart from Him, if nonetheless
His own.

Still, by the time anything so weakly theatrical as that has
occurred, already so many invisible preparations: God's general
availability, His brooding peckishness, an appetite and
predilection—even before invention—to invent, to give vent,
an all but unsuspected longing for desire followed by the
eventual arrival of desire's deep hum, its thrumming
escalation and upward flight into the dome's aperture, already
open and voluble and without warning giving voice.

But how long, and without benefit of time's secretarial skills,
had that Visage lain facing this direction? What hunger must

have built before the first repast? And, we might well ask, to what end, if any? And if any end, why begin? (The imagination's tedious mimesis of the sea.) In the incommensurate cathedral of Himself, what stillness!

What extreme expression could prevail against that self-same weight? And would such, then, be approximate to trinity? An organization, say, like this: The Enormity, Its Aspirations, Its Voice. Forever God and the mind of God in wordless discourse until that first polarity divests a shout against the void. Perhaps it is that first resounding measure which lays foundation for every flowing utterance to come. It would appear to us, I suppose, as a chaos of waters—and everything since proceeding from the merest drop of it.

So long as we have come this far, we may as well continue onto God's initial venture, His first concession at that locus out of time when He invented the absence of Himself, which first retraction avails for all the cosmos and for us. In the very midst of His unending wholeness He withdraws, and a portion of what He was He abdicates. We may suppose our entire aberration to proceed from that dislocated hand, and may suppose the terror we suspect—and which lingers if only to discourage too long an entertainment—to be the trace and resonance of that self-inflicted wound.

So why the vertiginous kiss of waters? Why the pouring chaos at our beginning which charges all that scene with . . . would you call it *rapture*? Perhaps the dawning impulse of our creation, meager as it may have been, pronounced—in terms we never heard—God's return.

Murmur

God Stammers with Us . . .

—CALVIN

What is this familiar pulse beginning
in the throat which promises to pronounce
for once the heart's severer expectations,
but which will not be articulated
from the glib, unhelpful mass of the tongue?

Late winter, the chill can go either way—
brief renewal, habitual decay.
Against our shore the sea extends again
its unrelenting question, and withdraws.
In such weather, the little boats stay put.

And who can blame them? This uncertainty
is the constant weather our horizon
employs to keep our expeditions brief
and—to the point—ineffectual,
while all the while the cliffs beneath us fail.

Still, the murmur of what the heart would like
finally to say, and so attain, repeats
our trouble: these little ventures with the tongue
are doomed by their very mode of travel.
The limits become what we cannot bear.

Dead Sea Bathers

What stillness their hearts must know, these bathers
laid out and glistening along the dissolve
of an ancient sea,

their bodies—so late from brief exercise,
so lately thrown down in exhaustion—
already marbled

with a fine white dust as they stretch across
straw pallets arranged by unseen servants
who, one supposes,

must see what we see. And how calm their thoughts,
these still brilliant shapes, as the mind's ebbing,
the heart's slow measure

lull the vessel and its oils, which now retard
to an all but breathless pace akin
to idiocy,

if saved from just that by the hum of faint
discomfort, that murmur beginning deep
as the flesh is fired.

The Turning of Lot's Wife

First of all, she had a name, and she had a history. She was *Marah*, and long before the breath of death's angel turned her to bitter dust, she had slipped from her mother's womb with remarkable ease, had moved in due time from infancy to womanhood with a manner of grace that came to be the sole blessing of her aging parents. She was beloved.

And like most daughters who are beloved by both a mother and a father, Marah moved about her city with unflinching compassion, tending to the dispossessed as if they were her own. And they became her own. In a city given to all species of excess, there were a great many in agony—abandoned men, abandoned women, abandoned children. Upon these she poured out her substance and her care.

Her first taste of despair was at the directive of the messengers, who announced without apparent sentiment what was to come, what was to be done. With surprising banality, they stood and spoke. One coughed into his fist and would not meet her eyes. And one took a sip from the cup she offered before he handed it back and the two disappeared into the night.

Unlike the man—coward and sycophant—the woman remained faithful unto death. For even as Lot fled the horrors of a city's conflagration, outrunning Marah and both girls as they all rushed into the desert, the woman stopped.

She looked ahead briefly to the flat expanse, seeing her tall daughters, whose strong legs and churning arms were taking them safely to the hills; she saw, farther ahead, the old man whom she had served and comforted for twenty years. In the impossible interval where she stood, Marah saw that she could not turn her back on even one doomed child of the city, but must turn her back instead upon the saved.

Disciplinary
Treatises

Disciplinary
Treatises

1. On the Holy Spirit

If, upon taking up this or any scripture,
or upon lifting your one good eye to inspect
the faintly green expanse of field already
putting forth its late winter gauze of grasses,

you come to suspect a hushed conversation
under way, you may also find sufficient grounds
to suspect that difficult disposition
we call the Ghost, river or thread drawn through us,

which, rippled as any taut rope might be, lifts
or drops us as if riding a wave, and which fends
off, for brief duration, our dense encumberment
—this flesh and its confusions—if not completely,

if only enough that the burden be felt, just
shy of crushing us.

2. *The Embarrassment of Last Things*

Already you smile, drop your eyes, and chew your cheek.
Centuries of dire prophecy have taught us all
to be, well, unconvinced. And there have been decades,
entire scores of years when, to be frank, wholesale

destruction didn't sound so bad, considering.
You remember; we were *all* disappointed.
That the world never ended meant we had to get
out of bed after all, swallow another dose

of stale breath with our coffee, scrape the grim ice
from our windshields one more time. On the way to work,
stuck in endless traffic, the radio or some
incredibly sincere billboard would promise us again

an end to this, and for a moment we almost
see it. But we know it's not an end, not really;
it's harder than that—some kind of strenuous chore
stretching out ahead like these stalled cars, showing our

general direction, inadvertently or not mocking our pace.

3. Sacraments

Doubtless, Grace is involved—when is it not?—but its
locus is uncertain, remains the cardinal
catch whenever we dare interrogate again
our sacramental dogma. After all, Grace may

lie, contracted, inaccessible in Yahweh's
ancient vault; and it could be these painstakingly
enacted tokens of mystery are really
about as good as paper money. But what if

even the troubled air we breathe were drenched above
our knowing with the golden balm of Adonai?
Well, I like to get carried away. Never mind
the wearied questions of which and how many dear

rituals may qualify; the dire attributes
of divine participation are what these days
could stand some specifics, or, say, a little more
dogmatic elucidation. For it may be

some dreadful portion—very God of very God—
makes periodic and discreet returns, piecemeal,
sabbatical visitation to a matter
and a territory absenced to suffer

our mutual and—let's face it—flagging venture.
But who knows? The Holy may flourish any form
figuring the self's diminishment,
any conjunctive ebbing which yields a reply.

4. The Communion of the Body

The Christ in his own heart is weaker
than the Christ in the word of his brother.
—DIETRICH BONHOEFFER

Scattered, petulant, argumentative,
the diverse members generally find
little, nothing of their own, to offer

one another. Like all of us, the saved
need saving mostly from themselves and so
they make progress, if at all, by dying

to what they can, acquiescing to this
new pressure, new wind, new breath which would fill
them with something better than their own good

intentions. Or schemes of community.
Or their few articulate innovations
in dogma. What the Ghost expects of them

is a purer than customary will
to speak together, a *mere* willingness
to hear expressed in the fragmentary

figures of one another's speech the mute
and palpable identity they share,
scoured clear of impediment and glare,

the uncanny evidence that here
in the stillest air between them the one
we call the Ghost insinuates his care

for the unexpected word now fondling
the tongue, now falling here, incredible
confession—that they would be believers,

who startle to suspect among the scraps
of Babel's gritty artifacts one stone,
irreducible fossil, capable

of bearing love's unprovoked inscription
in the locus of its term.

5. Angels

As with wine, one might tender an entire lifetime
with hierarchies and their array of habits,

characteristic chores, nearness to the Holy,
their special tricks. One might speculate their number.

And what has *not* been said about these our brothers?
So little of it reliable, so little

corresponding to the actual, to the pure
indifference with which most angels skim aloft

our understanding, either incapable
of seeing our distress, or not interested.

Still, stories—*never* verifiable—persist:
the fortunate warning, the inexplicable swerve.

These insinuate themselves against our better
judgment, provide comfort beyond apparent cause.

There are other stories, after all, more somber
accounts of angelic intercourse: How, by force

or guile, a woman or boy has been taken, made
an unwilling portal for some monstrosity

or one of many lies. This version I believe.
Angels are of two sorts; best not to provoke either.

6. Satan

And while we're on the subject of angels—
their dubious character, their famous
unreliability—we should pause

to examine the notorious, one-
time hero and major disappointment:
The Bright One, chief ingrate to the most high,

morning star, petty prince, *et cetera*.
Say what you dare, he still *is* somebody.
And, if ever I could open my eyes

sufficiently to see what the air is
full of, I might be torn by his glory
even now, even as it is: rebuked,

diminished, scoured raw unto an extreme
radiance, and I daresay I'd find my
knees, and cower there, and worship him, which

action would gain me a measure of his part.

7. *Baptism*

Of those first waters in which we rolled and swam oblivious
and from which we fled into this confusion of life and death,
here is a little picture. Granted the scheme has undergone
some modest accommodation for the sake of decorum,
practicality, and—who knows?—our unwillingness to risk
a chill, so that the symbolic return to Christ's dire tableau
is, well, less than obvious, and one might subsequently risk
infusing the elements themselves with a little magic.
No real harm there, probably, unless one is then disinclined
to appreciate a metaphor when it's poured in his face.

In the older way, then, the trembling primative would be led
into a river where he would likely hear some familiar
business about his being buried, whereupon he would
go under. What each receives at this point—underwater—is
fairly individual, pretty various, unlikely
to be written down. But then he is returned and, surfacing,
hears that he is raised in the likeness of a resurrection.
He swims in such affusions as he regains the littered shore.

8. Blood Atonement

This much we might say with some assurance:
a crucifixion occurred, apparently
gratuitous, but a harsh intersection—

tree and flesh and some iron. We might add
sufficient blood resulted to bring about
a death, the nature of which we still puzzle.

As to why? Why the blood? Why the puzzle?
It seems that no one who knows is saying,
which is not to say we lack opinion.

For while we suffer no shortage of dire
speculation, hardly any of it
has given us anything like a clue.

All we dare is that it was necessary,
that we have somehow become both culprit
and beneficiary, and that we

are left to something quite like a response
to that still lost blood, to the blameless world.

9. *Grace*

Long before you knew desire, Desire turned
to you, saw you as you are even now—
unlovely, a little embarrassed, dead.

Can you remember the throat's pure pulse first
waking you up to a longing you would
neither fix to a name, nor satisfy?

Probably not. But it must have happened.
For thereafter under the influence
of Desire's instruction, you made desire

the new light by which you would dare proceed,
and it has led you here, where you adopt
the drape of love's body and find your own.

10. A Recuperation of Sin

I suppose we might do away with words like *sin*.
They are at least archaic, not to mention rude,
and late generations have been pretty well schooled

against the presumption of holding *anything*
to be absolutely so, universally
applicable, especially anything like

sin which is, to put it more neatly, unpleasant,
not the sort of thing one brings up. Besides, so much
of what ignorance may have once attributed

to *sin* has been more justly shown to be the end
result of bad information, genetic flaw,
or, most often, an honest misunderstanding.

And I suppose *sin's* old usefullness may have paled
somewhat through many centuries of overuse
by corrupt clergy pointing fingers, by faithless

men and women who have longed more than anything
for a more rigid tyranny over their wives
and husbands, over their somnambulant children.

In fact, we could probably forget the idea
of sin altogether if it were not for those
periodic eruptions one is quite likely

to picture in the papers, or on the TV—
troubling episodes in which, inexplicably,
some giddy power rises up to occasion

once more the spectacle of the innocent's blood.

11. Pain

No new attempt at apology here:
All suffer, though few suffer anything
like what they deserve.

Still, there are the famous *un*deserving
whose pain astonishes even the most
unflinching disciples

whose *own* days have been consumed by hopeless
explanation for that innocent whose torn
face or weeping burns

or ravenous disease says simply *no,*
not good enough. This is where we must begin:
Incommensurate

pain, nothing you can hope to finger
into exposition, nothing you can
cover up. A fault

—unacceptable and broad as life—gapes
at your feet, and the thin soil you stand
upon is giving way.

12. *The End of Heaven and the End of Hell*

At long last the feeble fretwork tumbles
apart forever and you stand alone,
unprotected, undeceived, in fullness.
And we are all there as well, equally

alone and equally full of . . . Ourselves.
Yes, I believe Ourselves is what we then
become, though what *that* is must surprise
each trembling figure; and in horror

or elation the effect will be the same
humility, one of two discrete sorts,
perhaps, but genuine humility.
And that long record of our choices—your

every choice—is itself the final
body, the eternal dress. And, of course,
there extends before us finally a measure
we can recognize. We see His Face

and see ourselves, and flee. And shame—old
familiar—will sustain that flight unchecked,
or the Ghost, forgotten just now—merest
spark at the center—will flare, bid us turn

and flame unto a last consuming light:
His light, our light, caught at last together
as a single brilliance, extravagant,
compounding awful glories as we burn.

Late Epistle

And Also from the Son

—qui ex Patre filioque

As you might expect, my momentary vision barely
qualifies: you know, sensation something like the merest
swoon, some uncertainty about why all of a sudden
the back garden, its bamboo and rose, the reaching pecans
(one's apparent field contracting to a field of vision)
took to trembling, as well as other accompanying
uncanniness. I mean, *was* the garden trembling or had
it suddenly, unnaturally stopped? Was the disturbing
motion something I was seeing or something I was
seeing with? And why am I asking you?

Perhaps I'm not. Probably, the most I'm doing is one
kind of homage to a moment and a form, a rhetoric
disclaiming what the habitual senses can't make much of.
This is what I can vouch for: I was at rest in a still,
restful corner of our back garden. I had expected
even to doze, but instead found my attention fixing
all the more alertly on the narrow scene, and then I
wasn't seeing anything at all, which is why I'm less
than eager to call this business exactly a vision.
Does one ever *sink* into a vision?

Let's suppose one might. Once interred, what does one come
    to find?
I found the semblance of a swoon, and began to suspect
ongoing trouble at the heart, a fullness in the throat,
an expanding, treble note whose voice was neither mine alone
nor completely separate. I know enough to know you

cannot believe this, not if I were carelessly intent on saying it was *so*. It was a fiction which I chanced upon as evening overtook our walled back garden— whether by virtue of light's ebbing or the fortunate influx of approaching shade, who would say?

Late Epistle

Do thy diligence to return before winter.

Timotheus, late disciple of Christ,
bishop to a burlesque we call the church
at Ephesus, priest, sometime son of Paul.

To that Apostle, whose unsurprising
exhortations and rebukes have arrived
anew—this time imparted by the hand

of Tychicus, old sycophant and drudge.
Grace and peace and whatever else you'll have
from me, and from Him who accepts so much.

I, too, thank God—whom I serve, and without
coaxing—to hear you are well, if somewhat
inconvenienced by this latest Roman

holiday. Nero remains uncertain
as to what to make of you? Rest assured
he will think of something, and when he does

you will be reprieved of our annoying
insufficiency, and—let us be frank—
rid of the fear that we may get it wrong,

that we may take our liberties in Christ
too liberally—all the way to joy.
Yes, I *am* baiting you, but not to strife,

rather to a manner of repose you
might adopt as you would a broadcloth robe,
one with a little space for the body's

diversities each to entertain
a little breathing room. Yes, I suppose
I *have* learned a thing or two, most of which

I have gathered from your imprisoned self.
Let me teach these back to you, confident
you have the time to listen, unless our

Nero has become a far braver man
overnight, which is, I'd say, unlikely.
He'd sooner miss a meal than make a god

of Paul. So now, knowing your suffering,
knowing how even your celebrated
wits are tried by the saints' abandonment,

I risk pressing them further. Still, you might
recall *I* have never abandoned *you.*
So, in mock frustration, your ingrate son

presumes to counsel his venerable—
if lately a little vulnerable—
father. I suggest another likely

possibility regarding how we
belated, disorderly believers
fare at Ephesus: We are suspicious,

frankly, of the certainty you expect
to find among us. Of a morning, we
might arise and stand before our houses,

inclined to discover—as you seem to
discover—in the very road, or in
the field beyond the road, or in the curve

of the horizon some quieting calm
or promise. Instead, in those wavering
figures we recognize a general

solicitude which echoes the troubling,
irrepressible tremor of our thoughts.
As latecomers to the invisible,

we live within our doubt; one might say we
live *by* it, a custom you no longer
entertain, having witnessed your own doubt

snatched from your eyes along with a short-lived,
corrective blindness. So, as one forgoes
a little blindness, one may receive some,

perhaps, in turn. Let me become your eyes
in doubt, just as you have been mine in faith.
Unlike you—and the dwindling apostles

who claim to have seen him, touched him, to have
heard his very voice, witnessed thereafter
the death—we suffer a complicated

circumstance: the moment of such presence
has passed. At each remove—by now these are
countless—another occasion for error

avails another disruption of one's
faith in the integrity of the tale,
another opportunity for pure

elaboration, accidental lapse,
for deliberate (forgive me) deceit.
It is not enough that we dare trust God,

or trust the Christ—we must put faith in what
moves others, men and women like ourselves,
and like ourselves untrustworthy, confused,

given to wishful thinking. Moreover,
I propose it is not fear, exactly,
which compells me and which draws the saints

at Ephesus to the manner of care
we take in laying our testimony
before the lost—not, in any case, fear

of the mundane complexion you imply.
We are not ashamed of *Him*, not so much
as we've appeared, from time to time, of you.

We hold our faith as boldly as we can—
which is to say, we do not hold it well,
but must rely upon the palpable

reciprocity of the hidden Ghost,
an embarrassment one must take care
not to trifle with, which none would announce

to the mob—the thick and unrepentant
thugs with which our great city populates
its marketplace. Paul, they'd stone you here again,

which would give you Paradise, but earn them
something less—harder heads, deeper blindness,
but not trouble even for a moment

their acquiescence to the apparent
slop jars of their lives. So, at Ephesus
the timid saints proceed as if the blind

might one day be restored to a measure
of sight, at least to the obscurity
which will no longer satisfy itself

that *anything* is clearly seen. Call it doubt
that calls us from the dust at Ephesus,
that bids us walk, and speak, and listen all

the more intently to the words which we
exchange, wanting to hear within our own
surprising utterances the living

pulse we know as the only sound we dare
believe. Forgive us, Paul, if we cannot
quite imitate the figure of yourself.

Remember us once the darkened glass
dissolves, no longer clouds the clarity
of an object seen, of a spoken word.

In the meantime, what have we to do
but doubt the simple reductions of brutes,
savor the trembling aspects of ourselves.

Mortuary Art

Even the ancient, open gate—whose hinges may
as well be stone, whose purpose has always been
purely ornamental—rests extravagantly
at its protected terminus: black fleurs-de-lys
topping a Byzantine blaze of black ironwork.

Once inside, the live-oak- and ash-dappled expanse
of gaudy statuary seems infinite, spreads
far as you can see and, presumably, farther:
a great many winged forms, more or less angelic,
some bearing human burdens, others extending

arms in an open embrace, but all with the same
expressionless faces of weary dockworkers.
Whichever narrow lane you choose, you find ahead
a multitude of crosses: Latin mostly, but
mingled with scores of Greek and Celtic, one or two

Pattée, Botonée, and down a lonely detour
the still, dire flames of one startling, spiny Maltese.
Pausing before any one of these explains
what time is for: lending weather its circumstance
for dissolving whatever it happens across.

All cemetery roads converge upon a center
where—dwarfed and nearly obscured by outsized,
marble masonry and a high ring of ancient
trees (so much like stone)—lies a brackish pool like tar.
Nothing lives in it: its waters compose a grim

accumulation of poisons laid out to keep
the foreground neat, deceptively green, natural.

Still, one is very likely to neglect the font
(so easy it's become to slight what isn't blemished),
and wander off, though the dust of the throat goes drier.

From the shallows of that ruined pool, a copper tube
—flanged at the lip, and no thicker than your finger—
blossoms out beyond its stem into something
of a calyx, or white anemone, a wavering
rush of water so pure you'll want to drink of it.

One imagines we need not confuse the fountain
with its pool any more than we need pretend
the gate, the angels, the scores of crosses partake
in our little stroll among the dead, or suffer
interest in our being here among them.

In that cove, water from the font leaps up, its foam
drawing light from some obscurity beyond the trees,
inviting all who have come this far to proceed
a little farther, to press their lips against
the rising pulse where all may drink or may withdraw.

Scott Cairns is an assistant professor of English and
director of the creative writing program at the University
of North Texas. He is the author of *The Theology of Doubt*
and *The Translation of Babel* (Georgia, 1990).

The Contemporary Poetry Series

EDITED BY PAUL ZIMMER

The Contemporary Poetry Series

EDITED BY BIN RAMKE